THREE DEATHS

BY

LYOF N. TOLSTOÏ

TRANSLATED FROM THE RUSSIAN

BY

NATHAN HASKELL DOLE

LYOF N. TOLSTOÏ

THREE DEATHS

A TALE.

1859.

I.

It was autumn.

Along the highway came two equipages at a brisk pace. In the first carriage sat two women. One was a lady, thin and pale. The other, her maid, with a brilliant red complexion, and plump. Her short, dry locks escaped from under a faded cap; her red hand, in a torn glove, put them back with a jerk. Her full bosom, incased in a tapestry shawl, breathed of health; her restless black eyes now gazed through the window at the fields hurrying by them, now rested on her mistress, now peered solicitously into the corners of the coach.

Before the maid's face swung the lady's bonnet on the rack; on her knees lay a puppy; her feet were raised by packages lying on the floor, and could almost be heard drumming upon them above the noise of the creaking of the springs, and the rattling of the windows.

The lady, with her hands resting in her lap and her eyes shut, feebly swayed on the cushions which supported her back, and, slightly frowning, struggled with a cough.

She wore a white nightcap, and a blue neckerchief twisted around her delicate pale neck. A straight line, disappearing under the cap, parted her blonde hair, which was smoothly pomaded; and there was a dry, deathly appearance about the whiteness of the skin in this simple parting. The withered and rather sallow skin was loosely drawn over her delicate and pretty features, and there was a hectic flush on the cheeks and cheek-bones. Her lips were dry and restless, her thin eyelashes had lost their curve, and a cloth travelling capote made straight folds over her sunken chest. Although her eyes were closed, her face gave the impression of weariness, irascibility, and habitual suffering.

The lackey, leaning back, was napping on the coach-box. The hired driver[1], shouting in a clear voice, urged on his four powerful and sweaty horses, occasionally looking back at the other driver, who was shouting just behind them in an open barouche. The tires of the wheels, in their even and rapid course, left wide parallel tracks on the limy mud of the highway.

The sky was gray and cold, a moist mist was falling over the fields and the road. It was suffocating in the carriage, and smelt of eau-de-cologne and dust. The invalid leaned back her head, and slowly opened her eyes. Her great eyes were brilliant, and of a beautiful dark color. "Again!" said she, nervously pushing away with her

---

1 *yamshchik.*

beautiful attenuated hand the end of her maid's cloak, which occasionally hit against her knee. Her mouth contracted painfully.

Matriósha raised her cloak in both hands, lifting herself up on her strong legs, and then sat down again, farther away. Her fresh face was suffused with a brilliant scarlet.

The invalid's handsome dark eyes eagerly followed the maid's motions; and then with both hands she took hold of the seat, and did her best to raise herself a little higher, but her strength was not sufficient.

Again her mouth became contracted, and her whole face took on an expression of unavailing, angry irony.

"If you would only help me.... Ah! It's not necessary. I can do it myself. Only have the goodness not to put those pillows behind me.... On the whole, you had better not touch them, if you don't understand!"

The lady closed her eyes, and then again, quickly raising the lids, gazed at her maid.

Matriósha looked at her, and gnawed her red lower lip. A heavy sigh escaped from the sick woman's breast; but the sigh was not ended, but was merged in a fit of coughing. She scowled, and turned her face away, clutching her chest with both hands. When the coughing fit was over, she once more shut her eyes, and continued to sit motionless. The coach and the barouche rolled into the village. Matriósha drew her fat hand from under her shawl, and made the sign of the cross.

"What is this?" demanded the lady.

"A post-station, madame."

"Why did you cross yourself, I should like to know?"

"The church, madame."

The lady looked out of the window, and began slowly to cross herself, gazing with all her eyes at the great village church, in front of which the invalid's carriage was now passing.

The two vehicles came to a stop together at the post-house. The sick woman's husband and the doctor dismounted from the barouche, and came to the coach.

"How are you feeling?" asked the doctor, taking her pulse.

"Well, my dear, aren't you fatigued?" asked the husband, in French. "Wouldn't you like to go out?"

Matriósha, gathering up the bundles, squeezed herself into the corner, so as not to interfere with the conversation.

"No matter, it's all the same thing," replied the invalid. "I will not get out."

The husband, after standing there a little while, went into the post-house. Matriósha, jumping from the carriage, tiptoed across the muddy road, into the enclosure.

"If I am miserable, there is no reason why the rest of you should not have breakfast," said the sick woman, smiling faintly to the doctor, who was standing by her window.

"It makes no difference to them how I am," she remarked to herself as the doctor, turning from her with slow step, started to run up the steps of the station-house. "They are well, and it's all the same to them. O my God!"

"How now, Eduard Ivánovitch," said the husband, as he met the doctor, and rubbing his hands with a gay smile. "I have ordered my travelling-case brought; what do you say to that?"

"That's worth while," replied the doctor.

"Well now, how about *her*?" asked the husband with a sigh, lowering his voice and raising his brows.

"I have told you that she cannot reach Moscow, much less Italy, especially in such weather."

"What is to be done, then? Oh! my God! my God!"

The husband covered his eyes with his hand.... "Give it here," he added, addressing his man, who came bringing the travelling-case.

"You'll have to stop somewhere on the route," replied the doctor, shrugging his shoulders.

"But tell me, how can that be done?" rejoined the husband. "I have done every thing to keep her from going: I have spoken to her of our means, and of our children whom we should have to leave behind, and of my business. She would not hear a word. She has made her plans for living abroad, as though she were well. But if I should tell her what her real condition is, it would kill her."

"Well, she is a dead woman now: you may as well know it, Vasíli Dmítritch. A person cannot live without lungs, and there is no way of making lungs grow again. It is melancholy, it is hard, but what is to be done about it? It is my business and yours to make her last days as easy as possible. It is the confessor that is needed here."

"Oh, my God! Now just perceive how I am situated, in speaking to her of her last will. Let come whatever may, yet I cannot speak of that. And yet you know how good she is."

"Try at least to persuade her to wait until the roads are frozen," said the doctor, shaking his head significantly: "something might happen during the journey."

"Aksiúsha, oh, Aksiúsha!" cried the superintendent's daughter, throwing a cloak over her head and tiptoeing down the muddy back steps. "Come along. Let us have a

look at the Shirkínskaya lady: they say she's got lung-
trouble, and they're taking her abroad. I never saw how
any one looked in consumption."

Aksiúsha jumped down from the door-sill; and the two
girls, hand in hand, hurried out of the gates. Shortening
their steps, they walked by the coach, and stared in at the
lowered window. The invalid bent her head toward
them; but when she saw their inquisitiveness, she
frowned and turned away.

"Oh, de-e-ar!" said the superintendent's daughter,
vigorously shaking her head.... "How wonderfully pretty
she used to be, and how she has changed! It is terrible!
Did you see? Did you see, Aksiúsha?"

"Yes, but how thin she is!" assented Aksiúsha. "Let us
go by and look again; we'll make believe go to the well.
Did you see, she turned away from us; still I got a good
view of her. Isn't it too bad, Masha?"

"Yes, but what terrible mud!" replied Masha, and both of
them started to run back within the gates.

"It's evident that I have become a fright," thought the
sick woman.... "But we must hurry, hurry, and get
abroad, and there I shall soon get well."

"Well, and how are you, my dear?" inquired the
husband, coming to the carriage with still a morsel of
something in his mouth.

"Always one and the same question," thought the sick

9

woman, "and he's even eating!"

"It's no consequence," she murmured between her teeth.

"Do you know, my dear, I am afraid that this journey in such weather will only make you worse. Eduard Ivánovitch says the same thing. Hadn't we better turn back?"

She maintained an angry silence.

"The weather will improve maybe, the roads will become good, and that would be better for you; then at least we could start all together."

"Pardon me. If I had not listened to you so long, I should at this moment be at Berlin and have entirely recovered."

"What's to be done, my angel? it was impossible, as you know. But now if you would wait a month, you would be ever so much better; I could finish up my business, and we could take the children with us."

"The children are well, and I am ill."

"But just see here, my love, if in this weather you should grow worse on the road.... At least we should be at home."

"What is the use of being at home?... *Die* at home?" replied the invalid peevishly.

But the word *die* evidently startled her, and she turned upon her husband a supplicating and inquiring look. He dropped his eyes, and said nothing.

The sick woman's mouth suddenly contracted in a childish fashion, and the tears sprang to her eyes. Her husband covered his face with his handkerchief, and silently turned from the carriage.

"No, I will go," cried the invalid; and lifting her eyes to the sky, she clasped her hands, and began to whisper incoherent words. "My God! why must it be?" she said, and the tears flowed more violently. She prayed long and fervently, but still there was just the same sense of constriction and pain in her chest, just the same gray melancholy in the sky and the fields and the road; just the same autumnal mist, neither thicker nor more tenuous, but ever the same in its monotony, falling on the muddy highway, on the roofs, on the carriage, and on the sheep-skin coats of the drivers, who were talking in strong, gay voices, as they were oiling and adjusting the carriage.

II.

The coach was ready, but the driver loitered. He had gone into the driver's cottage[2], where it was warm, close, dark, and suffocating; smelling of human occupation, of cooking bread, of cabbage, and of sheep-skin garments.

Several drivers were in the room; the cook was engaged

---

2 *izbá.*

near the oven, on top of which lay a sick man wrapped up in pelts.

"Uncle Khveódor! hey! Uncle Khveódor," called a young man, the driver, in a tulup, and with his knout in his belt, coming into the room, and addressing the sick man.

"What do you want, rattlepate? What are you calling to Fyédka[3] for?" demanded one of the drivers. "There's your carriage waiting for you."

"I want to borrow his boots. Mine are worn out," replied the young fellow, tossing back his curls and straightening his mittens in his belt. "Why? is he asleep? Say, Uncle Khveódor!" he insisted, going to the oven.

"What is it?" a weak voice was heard saying, and a blowsy, emaciated face was lifted up from the oven.

A broad, gaunt hand, bloodless and covered with hairs, pulled up his overcoat over the dirty shirt that covered his bony shoulder. "Give me something to drink, brother; what is it you want?"

The young fellow handed him a small dish of water.

"I say, Fyédya," said he, hesitating, "I reckon you won't

---

3 Fyédka and Fyédya are diminutives
of Feódor, Theodore.

want your new boots now; let me have them? Probably you won't need them any more."

The sick man dropping his weary head down to the lacquered bowl, and dipping his thin, hanging mustache in the brown water, drank feebly and eagerly.

His tangled beard was unclean; his sunken, clouded eyes were with difficulty raised to the young man's face. When he had finished drinking, he tried to raise his hand to wipe his wet lips, but his strength failed him, and he wiped them on the sleeve of his overcoat. Silently, and breathing with difficulty through his nose, he looked straight into the young man's eyes, and tried to collect his strength.

"Maybe you have promised them to some one else?" said the young driver. "If that's so, all right. The worst of it is, it is wet outside, and I have to go out to my work, and so I said to myself, 'I reckon I'll ask Fyédka for his boots; I reckon he won't be needing them.' But maybe you will need them,—just say".…

Something began to bubble up and rumble in the sick man's chest; he bent over, and began to strangle, with a cough that rattled in his throat.

"Now I should like to know where he would need them?" unexpectedly snapped out the cook, angrily addressing the whole hovel. "This is the second month that he has not crept down from the oven. Just see how he is all broken up! and you can hear how it must hurt him inside. Where would he need boots? They would not think of burying him in new ones! And it was time long ago, God pardon me the sin of saying so. Just see how he chokes! He ought to be taken from this hovel to another, or somewhere. They say there's hospitals in the city; but what's you going to do? he takes up the whole room, and that's too much. There isn't any room at all. And yet you are expected to keep neat."

"Hey! Seryóha, come along, take your place, the people are waiting," cried the head man of the station, coming to the door.

Seryóha started to go without waiting for his reply, but the sick man during his cough intimated by his eyes that he was going to speak.

"You can take the boots, Seryóha," said he, conquering the cough and getting his breath a little. "Only, do you hear, buy me a stone when I am dead," he added hoarsely.

"Thank you, uncle; then I will take them, and as for the stone,—*éï-éï!*—I will buy you one."

"There, children, you are witnesses," the sick man was able to articulate, and then once more he bent over and began to choke.

"All right, we have heard," said one of the drivers. "But run, Seryóha, or else the stárosta will be after you again. You know Lady Shirkínskaya is sick."

Seryóha quickly pulled off his ragged, unwieldy boots,

and flung them under the bench. Uncle Feódor's fitted his feet exactly, and the young driver could not keep his eyes off them as he went to the carriage.

"*Ek!* what splendid boots! Here's some grease," called another driver with the grease-pot in his hand, as Seryóha mounted to his box and gathered up the reins. "Get them for nothing?"

"So you're jealous, are you?" cried Seryóha, lifting up and tucking around his legs the tails of his overcoat. "Off with you, my darlings," he cried to the horses, cracking his knout; and the coach and barouche with their occupants, trunks, and other belongings, were hidden in the thick autumnal mist, and rapidly whirled away over the wet road.

The sick driver remained on the oven in the stifling hovel, and, not being able to throw off the phlegm, by a supreme effort turned over on the other-side, and stopped coughing.

Till evening there was a continual coming and going, and eating of meals in the hovel, and the sick man was not noticed. Before night came on, the cook climbed upon the oven, and pulled off the sheep-skin from his legs.

"Don't be angry with me, Nastásya," murmured the sick man. "I shall soon leave you your room."

"All right, all right, it's of no consequence. But what is the matter with you, uncle? Tell me."

"All my innards are gnawed out, God knows what it is!"

"And I don't doubt your gullet hurts you when you cough so?"

"It hurts me all over. My death is at hand, that's what it is. *Okh! Okh! Okh!*" groaned the sick man.

"Now cover up your legs this way," said Nastásya, comfortably arranging the overcoat so that it would cover him, and then getting down from the oven.

During the night the hovel was faintly lighted by a single taper. Nastásya and a dozen drivers were sleeping, snoring loudly, on the floor and the benches. Only the sick man feebly choked and coughed, and tossed on the oven.

In the morning no sound was heard from him.

"I saw something wonderful in my sleep," said the cook, as she stretched herself in the early twilight the next morning. "I seemed to see Uncle Khveódor get down from the oven, and go out to cut wood. 'Look here,' says he, 'I'm going to help you, Násya;' and I says to him, 'How can you split wood?' but he seizes the hatchet, and begins to cut so fast, so fast that nothing but chips fly. 'Why,' says I, 'ain't you been sick?'—'No,' says he, 'I am well,' and he kind of lifted up the axe, and I was scared; and I screamed and woke up. He can't be dead, can he? —Uncle Khveódor! hey, uncle!"

Feódor did not move.

"Now he can't be dead, can he? Go and see," said one of the drivers who had just waked up. The emaciated hand, covered with reddish hair, that hung down from the oven, was cold and pale.

"Go tell the superintendent; it seems he is dead," said the driver.

Feódor had no relatives. He was a stranger. On the next day they buried him in the new burying-ground behind the grove; and Nastásya for many days had to tell everybody of the dream which she had seen, and how she had been the first to discover that Uncle Feódor was dead.

III.

Spring had come.

Along the wet streets of the city swift streamlets ran purling between bits of ice; bright were the colors of people's dresses and the tones of their voices, as they hurried along. In the walled gardens, the buds on the trees were bourgeoning, and the fresh breeze swayed their branches with a soft gentle murmur. Everywhere transparent drops were forming and falling....

The sparrows chattered incoherently, and fluttered about on their little wings. On the sunny side, on the walls, houses, and trees, all was full of life and brilliancy. The sky, and the earth, and the heart of man overflowed with youth and joy.

In front of a great seignorial mansion, in one of the principal streets, fresh straw was laid; in the house lay that same invalid whom we saw hastening abroad.

Near the closed doors of the house stood the sick lady's husband, and a lady well along in years. On a sofa sat the confessor, with cast-down eyes, holding something wrapped up under his stole[4]. In one corner, in a Voltaire easy-chair, reclined an old lady, the sick woman's mother, weeping violently.

Near her the maid stood holding a clean handkerchief, ready for the old lady's use when she should ask for it. Another maid was rubbing the old lady's temples, and blowing on her gray head underneath her cap.

"Well, Christ be with you, my dear," said the husband to the elderly lady who was standing with him near the door: "she has such confidence in you; you know how to talk with her; go and speak with her a little while, my darling, please go!"

He was about to open the door for her; but his cousin held him back, putting her handkerchief several times to her eyes, and shaking her head.

"There, now she will not see that I have been weeping," said she, and, opening the door herself, went to the

---

4 Called *epitrachilion* in the Greek Church.

invalid.

The husband was in the greatest excitement, and seemed quite beside himself. He started to go over to the old mother, but after taking a few steps he turned around, walked the length of the room, and approached the priest.

The priest looked at him, raised his brows toward heaven, and sighed. The thick gray beard also was lifted and fell again.

"My God! my God!" said the husband.

"What can you do?" exclaimed the confessor, sighing and again lifting up his brows and beard, and letting them drop.

"And the old mother there!" exclaimed the husband, almost in despair. "She will not be able to endure it. You see, she loved her so, she loved her so, that she.... I don't know. You might try, holy father[5], to calm her a little, and persuade her to go away."

The confessor arose and went over to the old lady.

"It is true, no one can appreciate a mother's heart," said he, "but God is compassionate."

The old lady's face was suddenly convulsed, and a hysterical sob shook her frame.

---

5 *bátiushka.*

"God is compassionate," repeated the priest, when she had grown a little calmer. "I will tell you, in my parish there was a sick man, and much worse than Márya Dmítrievna, and he, though he was only a shopkeeper[6], was cured in a very short time, by means of herbs. And this very same shopkeeper is now in Moscow. I have told Vasíli Dmítrievitch about him; it might be tried, you know. At all events, it would satisfy the invalid. With God, all things are possible."

"No, she won't get well," persisted the old lady. "Why should God have taken her, and not me?"

And again the hysterical sobbing overcame her so violently that she fainted away.

The invalid's husband hid his face in his hands, and rushed from the room.

In the corridor the first person whom he met was a six-year-old boy, who was chasing his little sister with all his might and main.

"Do you bid me take the children to their mamma?" inquired the nurse.

"No, she is not able to see them. They distract her."

The lad stopped for a moment, and after looking eagerly

---

6 *meshchánin.*

into his father's face, he cut a dido with his leg, and with merry shouts ran on. "I'm playing she's a horse, papásha," cried the little fellow, pointing to his sister.

Meantime, in the next room, the cousin had taken her seat near the sick woman, and was skilfully bringing the conversation by degrees round so as to prepare her for the thought of death. The doctor stood by the window, mixing some draught.

The invalid in a white dressing-gown, all surrounded by cushions, was sitting up in bed, and gazed silently at her cousin.

"Ah, my dear!" she exclaimed, unexpectedly interrupting her, "don't try to prepare me; don't treat me like a little child! I am a Christian woman. I know all about it. I know that I have not long to live; I know that if my husband had heeded me sooner, I should have been in Italy, and possibly, yes probably, should have been well by this time. They all told him so. But what is to be done? it's as God saw fit. We all of us have sinned, I know that; but I hope in the mercy of God, that all will be pardoned, ought to be pardoned. I am trying to sound my own heart. I also have committed many sins, my love. But how much I have suffered in atonement! I have tried to bear my sufferings patiently".....

"Then shall I have the confessor come in, my love? It will be all the easier for you, after you have been absolved," said the cousin.

The sick woman dropped her head in token of assent. "O God! pardon me a sinner," she whispered.

The cousin went out, and beckoned to the confessor. "She is an angel," she said to the husband, with tears in her eyes. The husband wept. The priest went into the sick-room; the old lady still remained unconscious, and in the room beyond all was perfectly quiet. At the end of five minutes the confessor came out, and, taking off his stole, arranged his hair.

"Thanks be to the Lord, she is calmer now," said he. "She wishes to see you."

The cousin and the husband went to the sick-room. The invalid, gently weeping, was gazing at the images.

"I congratulate you, my love," said the husband.

"Thank you. How well I feel now! what ineffable joy I experience!" said the sick woman, and a faint smile played over her thin lips. "How merciful God is! Is it not so? He is merciful and omnipotent!" And again with an eager prayer she turned her tearful eyes towards the holy images.

Then suddenly something seemed to occur to her mind. She beckoned to her husband.

"You are never willing to do what I desire," said she in a weak and querulous voice.

The husband, stretching his neck, listened to her

submissively.

"What is it, my love?"

"How many times I have told you that these doctors don't know any thing! There are uneducated women doctors: they make cures. That's what the good father said.... A shopkeeper.... send for him"....

"For whom, my love?"

"Good heavens! you can never understand me." And the dying woman frowned, and closed her eyes.

The doctor came to her, and took her hand. Her pulse was evidently growing feebler and feebler. He made a sign to the husband. The sick woman remarked this gesture, and looked around in fright. The cousin turned away to hide her tears.

"Don't weep, don't torment yourselves on my account," said the invalid. "That takes away from me my last comfort."

"You are an angel!" exclaimed the cousin, kissing her hand.

"No, kiss me here. They only kiss the hands of those who are dead. My God! my God!"

That same evening the sick woman was a corpse, and the corpse in the coffin lay in the parlor of the great mansion. In the immense room, the doors of which were closed, sat the clerk[7], and with a monotonous voice read the Psalms of David through his nose.

The bright glare from the wax candles in the lofty silver candelabra fell on the white brow of the dead, on the heavy waxen hands, on the stiff folds of the cerement which brought out into awful relief the knees and the feet.

The clerk, not varying his tones, continued to read on steadily, and in the silence of the chamber of death his words rang out and died away. Occasionally from distant rooms came the voice of children and their romping.

"*Thou hidest thy face, they are troubled; thou takest away their breath, they die and return to their dust.*

"*Thou sendest forth thy Spirit, they are created; and thou renewest the face of the earth.*

"*The glory of the Lord shall endure forever: the Lord shall rejoice in his works.*"

The face of the dead was stern and majestic. But there was no motion either on the pure cold brow, or the firmly closed lips. She was all attention. But did she perhaps now understand these grand words?

––––––––––

7 *diachók.*

IV.

At the end of a month, over the grave of the dead a stone chapel was erected. Over the driver's there was as yet no stone, and only the fresh green grass sprouted over the mound that served as the sole record of the past existence of a man.

"It will be a sin and a shame, Seryóha," said the cook at the station-house one day, "if you don't buy a gravestone for Khveódor. You kept saying, 'It's winter, winter,' but now why don't you keep your word? I heard it all. He has already come back once to ask why you don't do it; if you don't buy him one, he will come again, he will choke you."

"Well, now, have I denied it?" urged Seryóha. "I am going to buy him a stone, as I said I would. I can get one for a ruble and a half. I have not forgotten about it; I'll have to get it. As soon as I happen to be in town, then I'll buy him one."

"You ought at least to put up a cross, that's what you ought to do," said an old driver. "It isn't right at all. You're wearing those boots now."

"Yes. But where could I get him a cross? You wouldn't want to make one out of an old piece of stick, would you?"

"What is that you say? Make one out of an old piece of stick? No; take your axe, go out to the wood a little earlier than usual, and you can hew him out one. Take a little ash-tree, and you can make one. You can have a covered cross. If you go then, you won't have to give the watchman a little drink of vodka. One doesn't want to give vodka for every trifle. Now, yesterday I broke my axletree, and I go and hew out a new one of green wood. No one said a word."

Early the next morning, almost before dawn, Seryóha took his axe, and went to the wood.

Over all things hung a cold, dead veil of falling mist, as yet untouched by the rays of the sun.

The cast gradually grew brighter, reflecting its pale light over the vault of heaven still covered by light clouds. Not a single grass-blade below, not a single leaf on the topmost branches of the tree-top, waved. Only from time to time could be heard the sounds of fluttering wings in the thicket, or a rustling on the ground broke in upon the silence of the forest.

Suddenly a strange sound, foreign to this nature, resounded and died away at the edge of the forest. Again the noise sounded, and was monotonously repeated again and again, at the foot of one of the ancient, immovable trees. A tree-top began to shake in an extraordinary manner; the juicy leaves whispered something; and the warbler, sitting on one of the branches, flew off a couple of times with a shrill cry, and, wagging its tail, finally perched on another tree.

The axe rang more and more frequently; the white chips, full of sap, were scattered upon the dewy grass, and a slight cracking was heard beneath the blows.

The tree trembled with all its body, leaned over, and quickly straightened itself with a fearful shudder on its base.

For an instant all was still, then once more the tree bent over; a crash was heard in its trunk; and tearing the thicket, and dragging down the branches, it plunged toward the damp earth.

The noise of the axe and of footsteps ceased.

The warbler uttered a cry, and flew higher. The branch which she grazed with her wings shook for an instant, and then came to rest like all the others with their foliage.

The trees, more joyously than ever, extended their branches over the new space that had been made in their midst.

The first sunbeams, breaking through the cloud, gleamed in the sky, and shone along the earth and heavens.

The mist, in billows, began to float along the hollows; the dew, gleaming, played on the green foliage; translucent white clouds hurried along their azure path.

The birds hopped about in the thicket, and, as though beside themselves, voiced their happiness; the juicy leaves joyfully and contentedly whispered on the tree-tops; and the branches of the living trees slowly and majestically waved over the dead and fallen tree.